Baseball
Activity Book

A. B. C.

Tony J. Tallarico

DOVER PUBLICATIONS, INC.
Mineola, New York

Bibliographical Note

Baseball Activity Book is a new work, first published by
Dover Publications, Inc., in 2010.

International Standard Book Number
ISBN-13: 978-0-486-47387-1
ISBN-10: 0-486-47387-2

Manufactured in the United States by Courier Corporation
47387204
www.doverpublications.com

Note

If you're a baseball fan—or are simply interested in learning about America's "national pastime"—you will find plenty of fun in this fact-filled book. There are word-searches, mazes, codes, find-the-differences, and many other challenging puzzles. Learn when the first Major League Baseball night game was held, who wore the first catcher's mask, how much an official baseball weighs, and dozens of other fascinating facts. Are you ready for the first pitch? Let's get started!

Emmett Littleton Ashford was a Major League umpire from 1966 to 1970. Unlike other umpires at the time, he exaggerated his calls with exciting gestures. What else was unique about Ashford?

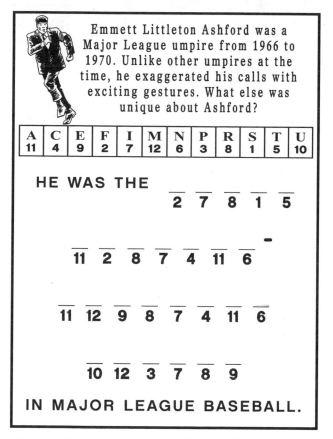

A	C	E	F	I	M	N	P	R	S	T	U
11	4	9	2	7	12	6	3	8	1	5	10

HE WAS THE __ __ __ __ __
                2 7 8 1 5

__ __ __ __ __ __ __ -
11 2 8 7 4 11 6

__ __ __ __ __ __ __ __
11 12 9 8 7 4 11 6

__ __ __ __ __ __
10 12 3 7 8 9

IN MAJOR LEAGUE BASEBALL.

Use the chart to decode the clues and complete this baseball fact.

Everyone knows that Babe Ruth was a home-run-hitting outfielder for the Yankees. But did you know that he started out on the Red Sox playing a very different position?

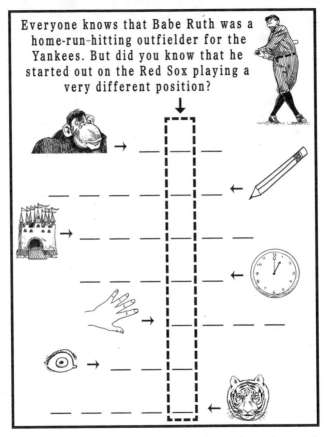

Write the name of each object pictured. One letter from each word will help spell the hidden answer.

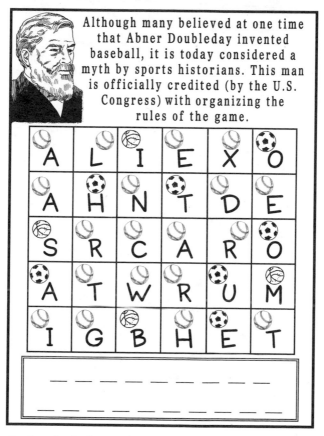

Although many believed at one time that Abner Doubleday invented baseball, it is today considered a myth by sports historians. This man is officially credited (by the U.S. Congress) with organizing the rules of the game.

A	L	I	E	X	O
A	H	N	T	D	E
S	R	C	A	R	O
A	T	W	R	U	M
I	G	B	H	E	T

Circle only the letters that are in a box with a baseball. List those letters, in the order they appear, to spell the name of baseball's organizer.

The Little League was started in 1939 as a three-team league in Pennsylvania. Today more than 2.3 million kids participate in Little League worldwide!

BATTER ○
CATCH ○
COACHES ○
FAIR ○
FUN ○
LEARN ○
PLAYERS ○
PRACTICE ○
RESPECT ○
RULES ○
SAFE ○
SPIRIT ○
TEACH ○
TEAMS ○
THROW ○
TRY ○

B A T E R C
T S R E Y A L P
Y R T H E R O W
E P E F C A L O
C L A R S A L R
I S M B A T E H
T H S P I R I T
C O A C H E S C
A N D S E T H E
R U L E S T F P
P F H C T A C S
E C I L I B A E
L U N R A E L R

Find and circle the words, listed above, that have something to do with Little League.

A baseball is covered with two strips of white horsehide (or cowhide) tightly stitched together. Approximately how much does an official baseball weigh?

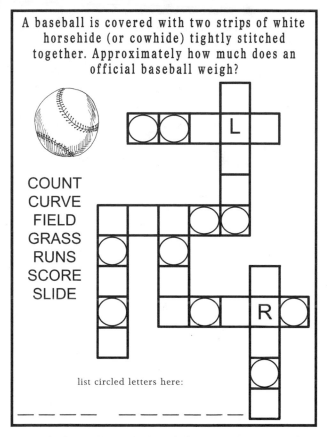

COUNT
CURVE
FIELD
GRASS
RUNS
SCORE
SLIDE

list circled letters here:

__ __ __ __ __   __ __ __ __ __

Write the baseball words, listed above, in the spaces where they belong in the puzzle. The circled letters, written in order, will spell the answer.

In 1910 it was discovered that a baseball with a cork center was livelier when hit. (Before this, balls were stuffed with feathers!)
The cork-center baseball is still used today in Major League Baseball.

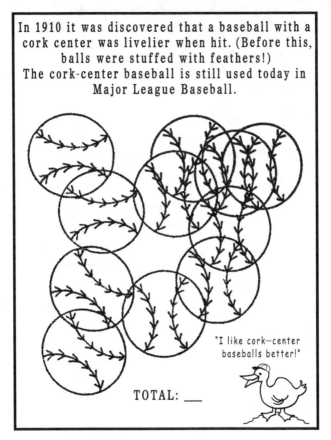

"I like cork—center baseballs better!"

TOTAL: ___

How many baseballs do you see on this page? Count carefully!

Although umpires aren't always a favorite of fans and players, they are an important part of the game. Umpiring goes back to 1876, when a man named William McLean became the first professional umpire. He umpired the very first game in National League history!

Find and circle the hidden objects in this cartoon. Use the checklist to keep track.

"Take Me Out to the Ball Game" is an early 20th century song that has become the unofficial anthem of baseball. Usually sung during a game's 7th-inning stretch, it was written by Jack Norworth and Albert Von Tilzer. What is strange about the song's authors?

OFJUIFS POF PG

UIFN BUUFOEFE

B HBNF CFGPSF

XSJUJOH UIF

TPOH !

Write the alphabet letter that comes before each of the letters in the spaces above. Then read the baseball fact.

An error is when a fielder misplays a ball and allows a batter or baserunner to reach one or more bases. The picture below is full of errors!

Can you find and circle eleven things that are wrong, or just don't belong, in this baseball scene?

The first night game in Major League Baseball was played in May 1935. The Reds beat the Phillies 2-1 at a ballpark in Cincinnati, Ohio.

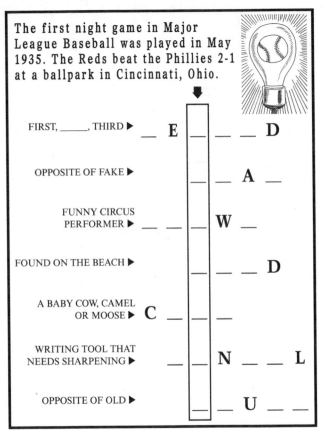

FIRST, ____, THIRD ▶ _ E _ _ _ D

OPPOSITE OF FAKE ▶ _ _ A _

FUNNY CIRCUS PERFORMER ▶ _ _ W _

FOUND ON THE BEACH ▶ _ _ _ D

A BABY COW, CAMEL OR MOOSE ▶ C _ _ _

WRITING TOOL THAT NEEDS SHARPENING ▶ _ _ N _ _ L

OPPOSITE OF OLD ▶ _ _ U _ _

To learn the name of the ballpark that hosted the first night game, complete the answers to the clues. One letter from each answer will help spell out the name.

The National Baseball Hall of Fame and
Museum was first dedicated in 1939.

ARTIFACTS ☐ **DISPLAY** ☐ **HISTORY** ☐ **HONOR** ☐
INDUCTEES ☐ **PRESERVE** ☐ **REPLICAS** ☐ **VISIT** ☐

S	Y	A	L	P	S	I	D
T	R	C	O	O	A	N	P
C	O	P	E	R	C	D	R
A	T	S	T	O	I	U	E
F	S	W	N	N	L	C	S
I	I	E	W	Y	P	T	E
T	H	O	R	K	E	E	R
R	O	N	O	H	R	E	V
A	V	I	S	I	T	S	E

___ _____ _____ ,

____ _____

Find and circle the baseball words hidden in the puzzle. The
remaining letters, written in the blanks in the order they
appear, will spell the location of the Hall of Fame.

11

Batting is considered one of the most difficult feats in sports. A batter must try to hit a small round ball (traveling very fast) with a thin round bat!

Find and circle, in the picture on the right, nine things that are different between these two pictures of Hall of Famer Mickey Mantle.

Nicknamed the "Eighth Wonder of the World," this domed stadium was the first of its kind.

KINGDOME
SEATTLE, WASHINGTON

ASTRODOME
HOUSTON, TEXAS

TROPICANA FIELD
ST. PETERSBURG, FLORIDA

To discover the first domed stadium, travel through this maze.

This Hall of Fame second baseman was the first African-American player in Major League Baseball.

Use a pencil to shade the areas that contain a STAR, and you will reveal the name of this historic player.

Unlike other sports that use a clock, baseball isn't controlled by a specific length of time. A typical baseball game is played in 9 innings.

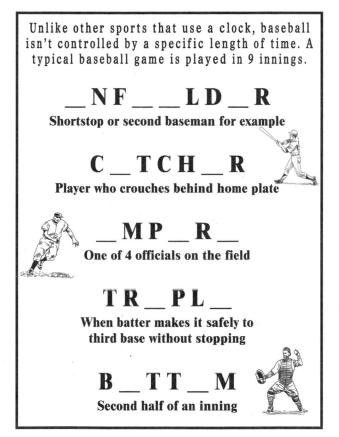

_ N F _ _ L D _ R

Shortstop or second baseman for example

C _ T C H _ R

Player who crouches behind home plate

_ M P _ R _

One of 4 officials on the field

T R _ P L _

When batter makes it safely to third base without stopping

B _ T T _ M

Second half of an inning

In the blanks, add the correct vowels to these baseball words. The clues can help you.

A women's professional baseball league existed from 1943 to 1954. The league had such teams as the Kenosha Comets, Racine Belles, and Rockford Peaches.

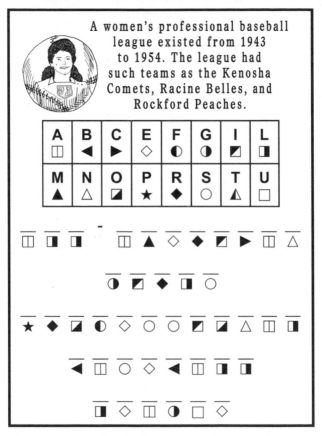

A	B	C	E	F	G	I	L
□	◀	▶	◇	◐	◑	◪	◨

M	N	O	P	R	S	T	U
▲	△	◪	★	◆	○	◭	□

Use the chart to decode the name of the women's professional baseball league.

The tradition of baseball in New York can be traced back to the days of the American Civil War! The nation's very first enclosed baseball field opened in New York City in May 1862.

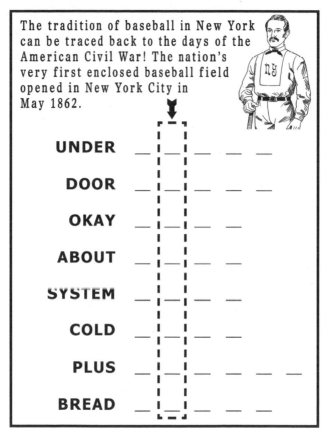

UNDER   _ _ _ _ _ _

DOOR   _ _ _ _ _

OKAY   _ _ _ _

ABOUT   _ _ _ _ _

SYSTEM   _ _ _ _ _ _

COLD   _ _ _ _

PLUS   _ _ _ _

BREAD   _ _ _ _ _

To find out where in New York this field was located, add these words to the puzzle grid in alphabetical order. Then read down the second column to reveal the answer.

Teams have used nicknames to identify themselves since the early days of baseball. One of the first recorded games took place between two teams simply called "New York" and "Knickerbockers."

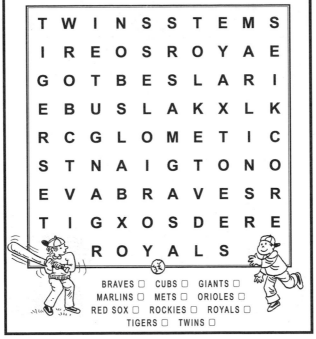

T	W	I	N	S	S	T	E	M	S
I	R	E	O	S	R	O	Y	A	E
G	O	T	B	E	S	L	A	R	I
E	B	U	S	L	A	K	X	L	K
R	C	G	L	O	M	E	T	I	C
S	T	N	A	I	G	T	O	N	O
E	V	A	B	R	A	V	E	S	R
T	I	G	X	O	S	D	E	R	E
	R	O	Y	A	L	S			

BRAVES ☐   CUBS ☐   GIANTS ☐
MARLINS ☐   METS ☐   ORIOLES ☐
RED SOX ☐   ROCKIES ☐   ROYALS ☐
TIGERS ☐   TWINS ☐

Find and circle the names of these eleven teams in the puzzle.

The Little League World Series was first held back in August 1947 in Pennsylvania. No matter where in the world the teams are from, this World Series is always played yearly in Pennsylvania.

The letter "W" is hidden nine times in this picture. Find and circle each "W."

A grand slam is a home run hit with the bases loaded. Who hit the most career grand slam home runs in Major League Baseball?

LOU GEHRIG

HANK AARON

SAMMY SOSA

Travel to the end of this maze to find out which player hit 23 career grand-slam home runs.

The Commissioner's Trophy is awarded each
year to the team winning the World Series.
First awarded in 1967, the flags on the trophy
represent each team currently in
Major League Baseball.

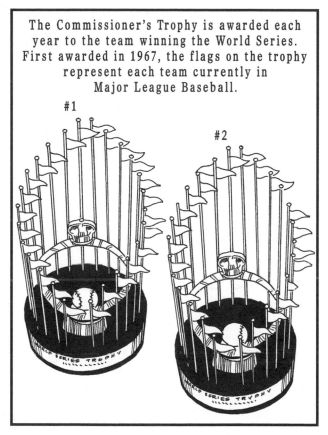

Are these two trophies identical? Look closely to find and
circle eight things that are different in trophy #2.

There are a few different throwing styles used by pitchers. The most common is an overhand delivery, but some pitchers use a sidearm or a submarine-style delivery.

BALL!

STRIKE!

WILD PITCH!

BALK!

Help this pitcher throw only a strike by successfully traveling to the end of this maze.

While the exact origin of baseball is unknown, most historians think that it is based on a sport that began in Ireland.

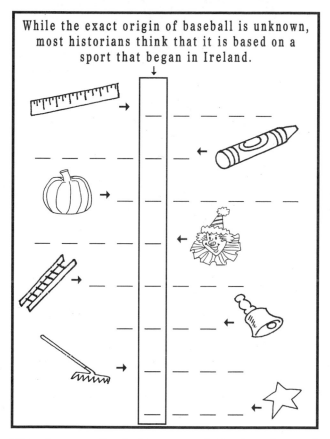

Write the name of each object pictured. One letter from each word will help spell the name of this nineteenth-century sport.

A batter should use a bat that is as tall as the player's hip when stood on the ground.

FOUL BALL

POP OUT

BASE HIT!

STRIKE

Help this batter get only a base hit by traveling through the maze. Be careful—or you might hit a foul ball!

A pitch is the act of throwing a baseball toward home plate to start a play. Pitchers throw many different types of pitches.

CHANGEUP ☐ CURVEBALL ☐
CUTTER ☐ FASTBALL ☐ FORKBALL ☐
SCREWBALL ☐ SINKER ☐ SLIDER ☐

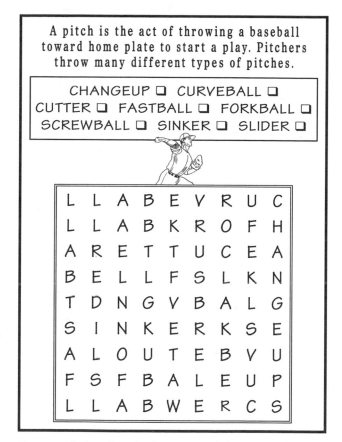

L	L	A	B	E	V	R	U	C
L	L	A	B	K	R	O	F	H
A	R	E	T	T	U	C	E	A
B	E	L	L	F	S	L	K	N
T	D	N	G	V	B	A	L	G
S	I	N	K	E	R	K	S	E
A	L	O	U	T	E	B	V	U
F	S	F	B	A	L	E	U	P
L	L	A	B	W	E	R	C	S

Can you find and circle the names of the types of pitches shown in the box above the puzzle?

Music is a common sound at sporting games - especially organ music at ballparks. The first organ debuted at a Major League ballpark in April 1941.

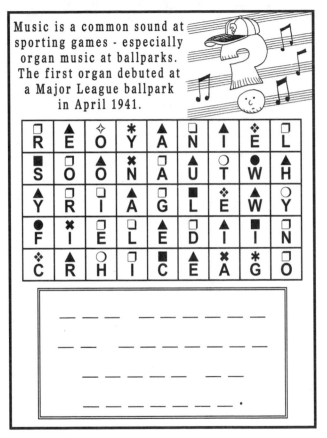

To find out who first played the organ at a Major League ballpark, cross out the letters that have a TRIANGLE. Write the remaining letters in order in the blank spaces.

Major League Baseball has a rule that "no one except players, substitutes, managers, coaches, trainers, and batboys shall occupy the dugout during a game."

BASEBALL ☐ FISH ☐ FLYING BAT ☐ FOOTBALL ☐
HOCKEY PUCK ☐ HOURGLASS ☐ PALM TREE ☐ PIE ☐
SCISSORS ☐ SCREWDRIVER ☐

Find and circle the hidden objects in this cartoon.

The four infielders are the first baseman, second baseman, shortstop and third baseman.

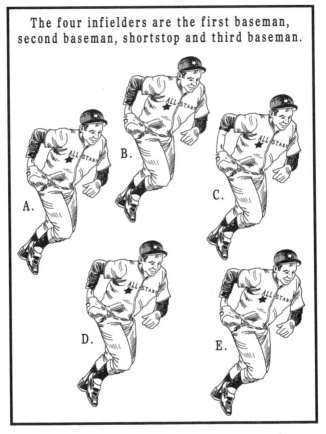

These infielders may look the same in every picture, but one is different from the others. Find and circle the infielder that is different.

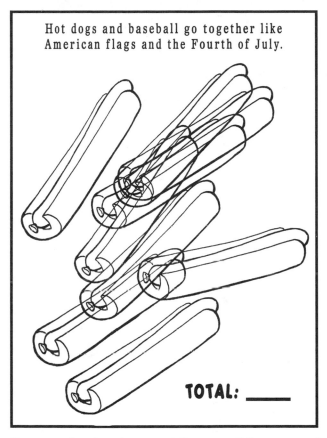

Hot dogs and baseball go together like American flags and the Fourth of July.

TOTAL: _____

How many hot dogs do you see? Count carefully, as some of them overlap.

Most team sports play on a rectangular field (like basketball and football). But baseball is played on a wedge-shaped field called a diamond.

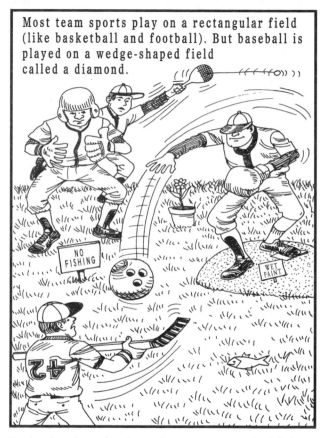

Find and circle twelve things that are wrong, or don't belong, on this baseball field.

A stadium is a place where an indoor or outdoor game of baseball can be played.

BASES
BULLPEN
DIAMOND
DUGOUT
ON DECK
SEATS

Write these words having to do with baseball stadiums in the correct spaces in the puzzle.

"B" is for baseball!

Find and circle fifteen things in this wacky baseball scene that begin with the letter "B."

Some of the first baseball trading cards were made in the late 1860s by a sporting goods company. The cards were used to advertise their products.

Today, collecting cards is still a popular hobby among sports fans.

Can you find and circle eight things that are different between these two silly baseball cards?

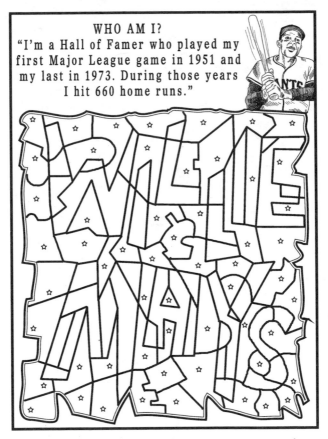

WHO AM I?
"I'm a Hall of Famer who played my first Major League game in 1951 and my last in 1973. During those years I hit 660 home runs."

Use a pencil to shade the areas that contain a STAR, and you will reveal the name of this baseball superstar.

The first Major League All-Star game was played on July 6, 1933, in Chicago. The American League won over the National, 4-2.

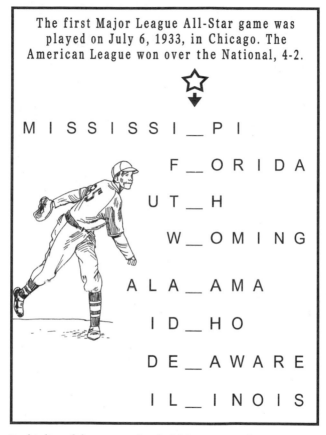

M I S S I S S I _ P I

F _ O R I D A

U T _ H

W _ O M I N G

A L A _ A M A

I D _ H O

D E _ A W A R E

I L L _ I N O I S

In this list of the names of eight U.S. states, each state is missing a letter. Fill in each name and then read down the starred column to discover a familiar phrase.

According to baseball history, a player named James Alexander was the first to wear a catcher's mask. He wore it during a game between Harvard students and the Live Oaks (a semipro team) in Massachusetts.

To learn in what year this took place, choose the correct path in the maze.

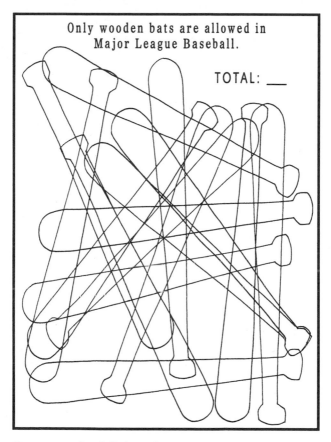

Only wooden bats are allowed in
Major League Baseball.

TOTAL: __

How many baseball bats do you see? Be sure to count
carefully.

It wasn't always "three strikes and you're out!"
In 1886 the number of strikes required for a
strikeout was four.

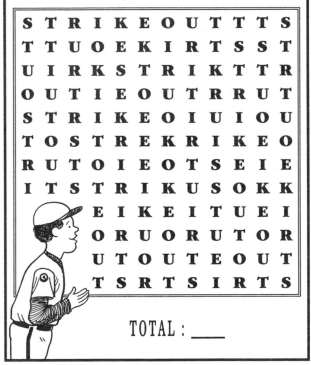

```
S T R I K E O U T T T S
T T U O E K I R T S S T
U I R K S T R I K T T R
O U T I E O U T R R U T
S T R I K E O I U I O U
T O S T R E K R I K E O
R U T O I E O T S E I E
I T S T R I K U S O K K
    E I K E I T U E I
    O R U O R U T O R
    U T O U T E O U T
    T S R T S I R T S
```

TOTAL : ____

How many times does the word STRIKEOUT appear in this
puzzle? Find and circle each one.

In order to throw a baseball accurately, your fingers should be placed over the top of the seams. This will give you a good grip.

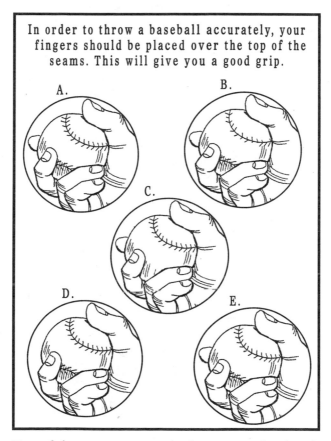

Two of the pictures are exactly the same. Find and circle them.

Every U.S. President since William Howard Taft has thrown out at least one ceremonial first ball or pitch, either for Opening Day, the All-Star Game, or the World Series. President Taft started the tradition on Opening Day in 1910 at Griffith Stadium, Washington, D.C.

#1   #2

Here are two pictures of President Taft. Find and circle six things in picture #2 that are different from picture #1.

In 1939, Yankee Lou Gehrig became the first player in baseball to have his uniform number retired.

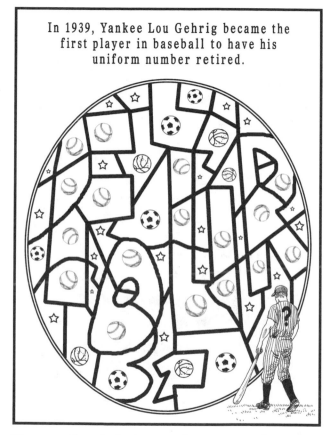

Use a pencil to shade the areas that contain only a BASE-BALL to reveal Gehrig's uniform number.

Do you have a favorite baseball player?

BONDS
CLEMENS
COOK
GARCIA
GLAVINE
HOWARD
JETER
JONES
LEE
MARTINEZ
ORTIZ
RAMIREZ
RIVERA
RODRIGUEZ
SANTANA
WEBB
WRIGHT

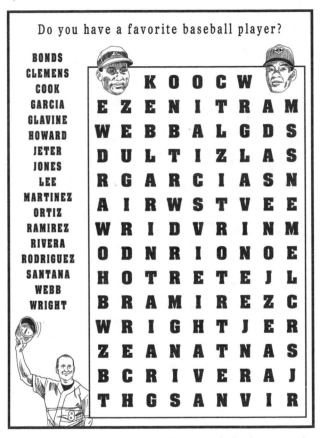

```
      K O O C W
E Z E N I T R A M
W E B B A L G D S
D U L T I Z L A S
R G A R C I A S N
A I R W S T V E E
W R I D V R I N M
O D N R I O N O E
H O T R E T E J L
B R A M I R E Z C
W R I G H T J E R
Z E A N A T N A S
B C R I V E R A J
T H G S A N V I R
```

Find and circle the names of these baseball players in the puzzle.

The Cy Young Award is given each year to the best pitchers in Major League Baseball, one each for the American and National leagues. The award is in honor of Hall of Fame pitcher Cy Young.

```
K O U F A X C
R H C O N E A
E Y N R S V R
V R D D W B L
A R E L Y L T
E E X A N U O
S P A H N E N
```

BLUE
CARLTON
CONE
FORD
KOUFAX
LYLE
PERRY
SEAVER
SPAHN
WYNN

Can you find the names of these Cy Young winners in the puzzle? Circle the names as you find them.

"Rainout," "rain delay" and "rain stopped play" are terms used when wet weather affects a baseball game.

I'm not afraid of a little rain!

N B K P S   M F B H V F

U F B N T   Q M B Z   J O

M J H I U   U P

N P E F S B U F   S B J O !

In each blank, write the alphabet letter that comes before each letter. Then read a statement about baseball and the weather.

The ancestor of the modern rounded-top baseball cap can be traced all the way back to 1860! Today it seems that everyone wears caps ... even if they're not playing baseball.

```
  S P A C
   P C P A
  C A C A P S
   S C P C S S
  C A S P A C
  S P A C P A
     C A P S
```

TOTAL: ___

How many times does the word CAPS appear in this puzzle? Circle each one and write the total.

The distance a baseball travels when hit
depends on the angle at which the ball leaves
the bat and how fast the ball is hit. What is a
hard-hitting batter in baseball often called?

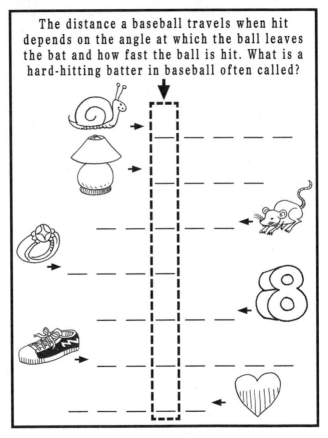

Write the name of each object pictured. One letter from each
word will help spell the answer.

Complete this maze to find the correct answer.

Can you solve this mystery picture?

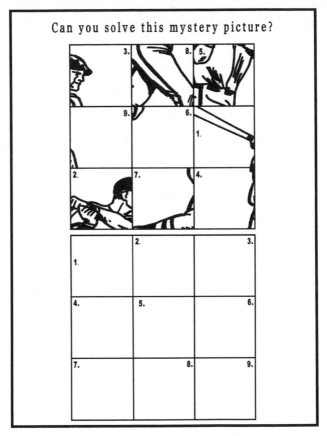

Draw exactly what you see in the top numbered boxes into the blank boxes of the same numbers below.

Solutions

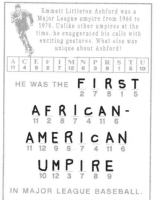

Emmett Littleton Ashford was a Major League umpire from 1966 to 1970. Unlike other umpires at the time, he exaggerated his calls with exciting gestures. What else was unique about Ashford?

A	C	E	F	I	M	N	P	R	S	T	U
11	4	9	2	7	12	6	3	8	1	5	10

HE WAS THE **F I R S T**
2 7 8 1 5

A F R I C A N -
11 2 8 7 4 11 6

A M E R I C A N
11 12 9 8 7 4 11 6

U M P I R E
10 12 3 7 8 9

IN MAJOR LEAGUE BASEBALL.

Page 1

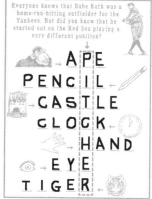

Everyone knows that Babe Ruth was a home-run-hitting outfielder for the Yankees. But did you know that he started out on the Red Sox playing a very different position?

A P E
PENCIL
CASTLE
CLOCK
HAND
EYE

TIGER

Page 2

Although many believed at one time that Abner Doubleday invented baseball, it is today considered a myth by sports historians. This man is officially credited (by the U.S. Congress) with organizing the rules of the game.

A L I E X O
A H N T D E
S R C A R O
A T W R U M
I G B H E T

ALEXANDER CARTWRIGHT

Page 3

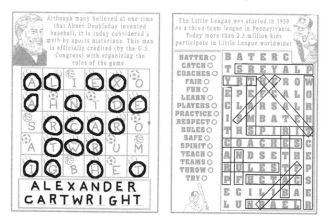

The Little League was started in 1939 as a three-team league in Pennsylvania. Today more than 2.3 million kids participate in Little League worldwide!

BATTER ○
CATCH ○
COACHES ○
FAIR ○
FUN ○
LEARN ○
PLAYERS ○
PRACTICE ○
RESPECT ○
RULES ○
SAFE ○
SPIRIT ○
TEACH ○
TEAMS ○
THROW ○
TRY ○

B A T E R C
T S R E Y A L P
Y R T O R O W
E P E F C A L O
C L R S A L R
L S M B A T H
H S P I R I T
C O A C H E S C
A N D S E T H E
P R U L E S M
P F H C T C S
E C I L B A E
L U N F A E L R

Page 4

49

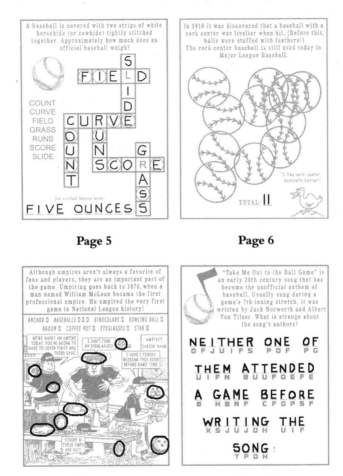

Page 5

A baseball is covered with two strips of white horsehide (or cowhide) tightly stitched together. Approximately how much does an official baseball weigh?

COUNT
CURVE
FIELD
GRASS
RUNS
SCORE
SLIDE

List circled letters here:

FIVE OUNCES

Page 6

In 1910 it was discovered that a baseball with a cork center was livelier when hit. (Before this, balls were stuffed with feathers!) The cork-center baseball is still used today in Major League Baseball.

"I like cork-center baseballs better!"

TOTAL: 11

Page 7

Although umpires aren't always a favorite of fans and players, they are an important part of the game. Umpiring goes back to 1876, when a man named William McLean became the first professional umpire. He umpired the very first game in National League history!

ANCHOR □ BASEBALLS □ □ □ BINOCULARS □ BOWLING BALL □ BROOM □ COFFEE POT □ EYEGLASSES □ STAR □

Page 8

"Take Me Out to the Ball Game" is an early 20th century song that has become the unofficial anthem of baseball. Usually sung during a game's 7th-inning stretch, it was written by Jack Norworth and Albert Von Tilzer. What is strange about the song's authors?

NEITHER ONE OF
THEM ATTENDED
A GAME BEFORE
WRITING THE
SONG

50

An error is when a fielder misplays a ball and allows a batter or baserunner to reach one or more bases. The picture below is full of errors!

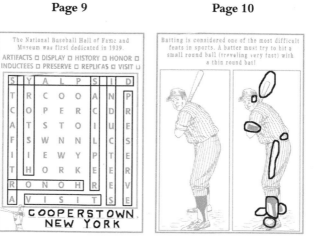

Page 9

The first night game in Major League Baseball was played in May 1935. The Reds beat the Phillies 2-1 at a ballpark in Cincinnati, Ohio.

FIRST, _____, THIRD ▶ S E **C O N** D

OPPOSITE OF FAKE ▶ R E A L

FUNNY CIRCUS PERFORMER ▶ C L O W N

FOUND ON THE BEACH ▶ S A N D

A BABY COW CAMEL OR MOOSE ▶ C A L F

WRITING TOOL THAT NEEDS SHARPENING ▶ P E N C I L

OPPOSITE OF OLD ▶ Y O U N G

Page 10

The National Baseball Hall of Fame and Museum was first dedicated in 1939.
ARTIFACTS ☐ DISPLAY ☐ HISTORY ☐ HONOR ☐
INDUCTEES ☐ PRESERVE ☐ REPLICAS ☐ VISIT ☐

S	Y	A	L	P	S	I	D	
T	R	C	O	O	A	N		P
C	O	P	E	R	C	I		R
A	S	T	O	I	L	C		E
F	W	N	N	L	P	T		S
I	I	E	W	Y	Y	E		E
T	H	O	R	K	E	E		R
R	O	N	O	H		R		V
A	V	I	S	I	T	S		E

COOPERSTOWN, NEW YORK

Page 11

Batting is considered one of the most difficult feats in sports. A batter must try to hit a small round ball (traveling very fast) with a thin round bat!

Page 12

Nicknamed the "Eighth Wonder of the World," this domed stadium was the first of its kind.

KINGDOME
SEATTLE, WASHINGTON

ASTRODOME
HOUSTON, TEXAS

TROPICANA FIELD
St. Petersburg, FLORIDA

Page 13

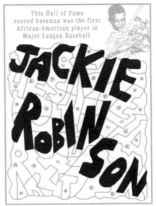

This Hall of Fame second baseman was the first African-American player in Major League Baseball.

JACKIE ROBINSON

Page 14

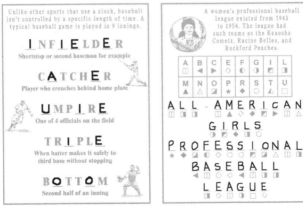

Unlike other sports that use a clock, baseball isn't controlled by a specific length of time. A typical baseball game is played in 9 innings.

INFIELDER
Shortstop or second baseman for example

CATCHER
Player who crouches behind home plate

UMPIRE
One of 4 officials on the field

TRIPLE
When batter makes it safely to third base without stopping

BOTTOM
Second half of an inning

Page 15

A women's professional baseball league existed from 1943 to 1954. The league had such teams as the Kenosha Comets, Racine Belles, and Rockford Peaches.

A	B	C	E	F	G	I	L
M	N	O	P	R	S	T	U

ALL-AMERICAN

GIRLS

PROFESSIONAL

BASEBALL

LEAGUE

Page 16

Page 17

The tradition of baseball in New York can be traced back to the days of the American Civil War! The nation's very first enclosed baseball field opened in New York City in May 1862.

UNDER   A B O U T

DOOR   B R E A D

OKAY   C O L D

ABOUT   D O O R

SYSTEM   O K A Y

COLD   P L U S

PLUS   S Y S T E M

BREAD   U N D E R

Page 17

Page 18

Teams have used nicknames to identify themselves since the early days of baseball. One of the first recorded games took place between two teams simply called "New York" and "Knickerbockers."

T	W	I	N	S	S	T	E	M	S		S
I		R	E	O	S		R	O	Y	A	E
G	O	T	B	E	S	L	A	R		I	I
E	B	U	S	L	A	K	X	L		K	K
R	C	G	L	O	M	E	T	I		C	C
S	T	N	A	I	G	T	O	N		O	
E	V	A		B	R	A	V	E	S		R
T	I	G	X	O	S	D	E	R	E		
			R	O	Y	A	L	S			

BRAVES ☐ CUBS ☐ GIANTS ☐
MARLINS ☐ METS ☐ ORIOLES ☐
RED SOX ☐ ROCKIES ☐ ROYALS ☐
TIGERS ☐ TWINS ☐

Page 18

Page 19

The Little League World Series was first held back in August 1947 in Pennsylvania. No matter where in the world the teams are from, this World Series is always played yearly in Pennsylvania.

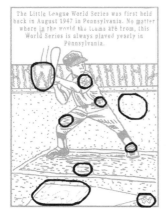

Page 19

Page 20

A grand slam is a home run hit with the bases loaded. Who hit the most career grand slam home runs in Major League Baseball?

LOU GEHRIG

HANK AARON

SAMMY SOSA

Page 20

The Commissioner's Trophy is awarded each year to the team winning the World Series. First awarded in 1967, the flags on the trophy represent each team currently in Major League Baseball.

#1

#2

Page 21

There are a few different throwing styles used by pitchers. The most common is an overhand delivery, but some pitchers use a sidearm or a submarine style delivery.

BALL!

STRIKE!

WILD PITCH!

BALK!

Page 22

While the exact origin of baseball is unknown, most historians think that it is based on a sport that began in Ireland.

RULER

CRAYON

PUMPKIN

CLOWN

LADDER

BELL

RAKE

STAR

Page 23

A batter should use a bat that is as tall as the player's hip when stood on the ground.

FOUL BALL

POP OUT

BASE HIT!

STRIKE

Page 24

54

Page 25

A pitch is the act of throwing a baseball toward home plate to start a play. Pitchers throw seven different types of pitches.

CHANGEUP ☐ CURVEBALL ☐ CUTTER ☐ FASTBALL ☐ FORKBALL ☐ SCREWBALL ☐ SINKER ☐ SLIDER ☐

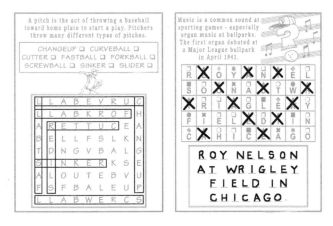

Page 26

Music is a common sound at sporting games - especially organ music at ballparks. The first organ debuted at a Major League ballpark in April 1941.

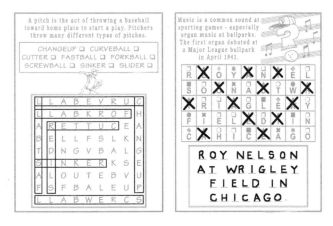

ROY NELSON AT WRIGLEY FIELD IN CHICAGO.

Page 27

Major League Baseball has a rule that "no one except players, substitutes, managers, coaches, trainers, and batboys shall occupy the dugout during a game."

BASEBALL ☐ FISH ☐ FLYING BAT ☐ FOOTBALL ☐ HOCKEY PUCK ☐ HOURGLASS ☐ PALM TREE ☐ PIE ☐ SCISSORS ☐ SCREWDRIVER ☐

Page 28

The four infielders are the first baseman, second baseman, shortstop and third baseman.

55

Hot dogs and baseball go together like American flags and the Fourth of July.

TOTAL: 9

Page 29

Most team sports play on a rectangular field (like basketball and football). But baseball is played on a wedge-shaped field called a diamond.

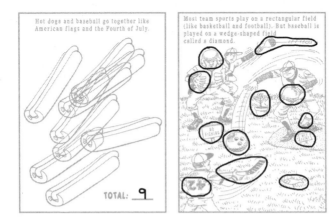

Page 30

A stadium is a place where an indoor or outdoor game of baseball can be played.

BASES
BULLPEN
DIAMOND
DUGOUT
ON DECK
SEATS

Page 31

"B" is for baseball!

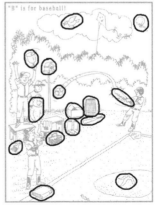

Page 32

Some of the first baseball trading cards were made in the late 1860s by a sporting goods company. The cards were used to advertise their products.

Today, collecting cards is still a popular hobby among sports fans.

Page 33

WHO AM I?
"I'm a Hall of Famer who played my first Major League game in 1951 and my last in 1973. During those years I hit 660 home runs."

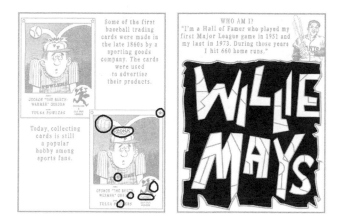

WILLIE MAYS

Page 34

The first Major League All-Star game was played on July 6, 1933, in Chicago. The American League won over the National, 4-2.

M I S S I S S I **P** P I
     F **L** O R I D A
    U T **A** H
   W **Y** O M I N G
  A L A **B** A M A
  I D **A** H O
 D E **L** A W A R E
I L **L** I N O I S

Page 35

According to baseball history, a player named James Alexander was the first to wear a catcher's mask. He wore it during a game between Harvard students and the Live Oaks (a semipro team) in Massachusetts.

I wish I had worn a mask.

1901

1897   1877

Page 36

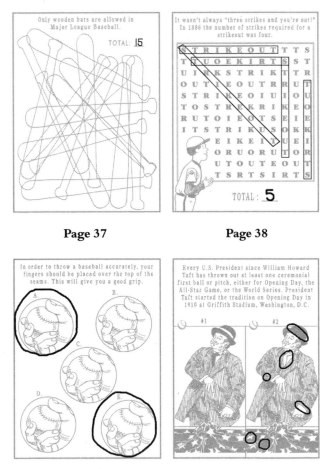

Only wooden bats are allowed in
Major League Baseball.

TOTAL: 15

It wasn't always "three strikes and you're out!"
In 1886 the number of strikes required for a
strikeout was four.

TOTAL: 5

Page 37

Page 38

In order to throw a baseball accurately, your
fingers should be placed over the top of the
seams. This will give you a good grip.

Every U.S. President since William Howard
Taft has thrown out at least one ceremonial
first ball or pitch, either for Opening Day, the
All-Star Game, or the World Series. President
Taft started the tradition on Opening Day in
1910 at Griffith Stadium, Washington, D.C.

Page 39

Page 40

Page 41

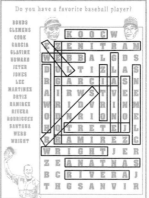

Page 42

Page 43

Page 44

SPAC
PCPA
CACAPS
SCPCSS
CASPAC
SPACPA
CAPS

TOTAL: 8

Page 45

SNAIL
LAMP
MOUSE
RING
EIGHT
SNEAKER
HEART

Page 46

BOSTON, MASSACHUSETTS
DETROIT, MICHIGAN
BALTIMORE, MARYLAND

START HERE!

Page 47

Page 48